BUSINESS FOR A BETTER WORLD

THE GEN Z GUIDE TO PROFIT AND PURPOSE

By Zachary Shapiro

Published by: Tapestry Intergenerational Education Foundation (TIEF)

ISBN: 979-8-9860574-3-9

Editor: Sophia Vlastupolo

Cover and book artwork by: Adrian Fisher Design Ltd, The Maze House, Durweston, Dorset, DT11 0QA, England

Design: Jim Baas

Printed by: IngramSpark

TABLE OF CONTENTS

Welcome to Business For a Better World!

I am excited to take you on a journey into the world of business, showing how it can help you in your everyday life and how we can work together to make the world a better place. I want to share how this book came to be.

It was the summer between 9th and 10th grade, and I had a job that kept me busy working at the checkout counter at our neighborhood grocery store. Although I still had plenty of free time each evening, I spent much of it playing video games with my friends. My father, who holds high expectations for me, wanted me to devote more time to academic goals. With this in mind, he gave me the choice: figure it out myself or figure it out with him.

Every family has their own thing. Some are lawyers, some are obsessed with animals, and others-like my own-love writing books. It may sound strange, but it's true. This love for writing has been passed down through generations, including my grandparents, father, and older brother, all of whom have written books. This inspired me to think about what I could write and how my journey could teach something valuable to others.

From a young age, I have always interested in owning a business and building something that could help myself and the world around me. I remember at age 9, I created a lemonade stand for people on the bike path near my house. The thrill of my first sale was unforgettable. I wanted to write about how I could carry this passion for creating useful products to help the world.

So, combining what I love most with my family's passion, I started generating ideas. I had never written a book before, so I turned to my Nana for guidance. She is an incredibly giving person, who will go out her way to make sure you thrive. And she mentored and supported me throughout this entire experience and I will never forget all her amazing help and wisdom. Our process was simple: I would write a chapter, she would read it and give me feedback, then I would revise it. It really helped solidify the book.

After about a year, working five days a week, two hours each day, I completed the first draft of Business for a Better World. I am so grateful to my grandparents for their love, support, and encouragement of my vision to write this book.

Next, I brought in a Gen Z editor, Sophia Vlastupolo, a brilliant college student who edited the book to improve clarity. Her perspective helped me see my work in new ways. Once I had a complete draft, I asked my dad if he would review it. We spent two hours each night sitting at the dining table editing each chapter. Over time, we streamlined the book, trimming it down to half its original length and focusing on the essentials.

I ran into a challenge: I had the content but lacked a publisher and guidance on how to distribute the book. My Nana, a health educator and author, introduced me to an amazing non-profit organization dedicated to supporting the mental health of teachers and students. The non-profit is called Tapestry Intergenerational Education Foundation (TIEF). With their help, I began speaking weekly with Professor Baas, the organization's president. She generously helped me clarify my ideas and define my goals. She even invited me to publish the book through TIEF, which was a fantastic opportunity.

It turns out that on the TIEF board is Adrian Fisher, the world's leading maze creator, responsible for over 700 mazes in 42 countries. He is renowned for creating labyrinths for royal families and museums. I am honored that he designed special mazes to illustrate the ideas in my book.

To make this a full family project, I also interviewed my grandfather, who led a dress company in Pennsylvania for many years; parts of that interview are included in the book.

With all this support, I want to deeply thank my family, especially my Mom, Dad, and brothers, and the TIEF organization for backing my ideas and my book. A special thanks to Dr. Sally A. Baas, TIEF President, who mentored me throughout this process. I am forever thankful. I also appreciate Jim Baas, who helped turn my chapters into a well-designed, user-friendly book.

Creating this book has been a rewarding journey, and I am grateful to the many incredible people who guided me along the way. This is my first book, and trust me, it took more work than I expected!

FOREWORD

By Dr. Sally A. Baas

President, Tapestry Intergenerational Education Foundation &
Former President, National Association of School Psychologists

This remarkable book is written by a student, age seventeen, and sponsored by a nonprofit called *Tapestry Intergenerational Education Foundation* (TIEF), whose purpose is to provide teachers and students with the tools they need to improve their well-being and build a sense of belonging within educational settings. Zachary brings to life a critical insight: *Business is not just for business people. It involves essential skills that we all need in order to thrive in society.*

This book empowers students to have a positive approach to business and to learn essential tools for critical thinking, collaboration, healthy communication, and creativity. These are skills that unite our students and bring entrepreneurship into focus for its value in making the world a better place..

Zachary has written this book through our nonprofit because we are investing in the voice of youth to help all of us understand how to thrive in our world. The students who are Gen Z have had a difficult path. Since mid-2020, they have been traumatized by the pandemic and the traumas of violence, war, and catastrophic events. There is a need to help them enhance their understanding of themselves and those around them. They also are dealing with loneliness and depression so there is a need for them to develop a sense of belonging.

Addressing these issues is challenging because there is reduced access to mental health services and caseloads are overwhelmed in educational contexts. There are not enough psychologists or mental health professionals to address these vast needs. So what should be done? There is a resource that I believe is incredibly under-utilized: the students themselves. Who is better situated to address this situation than the students themselves?

This book gives the students of Gen Z a voice in their own futures. And since business, as Zach says in the book, is for everyone, he offers powerful tools to help his generation flourish. He is an optimist at heart and shows this next generation a path for making the world a better place.

Through the eyes of a teenager, we get to understand how the Gen Z population views business and how they can create a healthy climate directly into their environment that leads toward positive individual and civic change.

This book addresses student well-being in a way that meets the students of Gen Z. It is based on the characteristics of those born into the Gen Z world, and its focus is on how to make business work for everyone. It involves the need for social interaction and healthy competition. Students learn through exploring the concepts of business to their real world. It engages the students in a meaningful way to them.

Zachary has done his homework and researched the business world of today and how he sees its growth as a Gen Z. Written in their language and edited by another Gen Z, Sofia Vlastopulo, you as readers will get the message that many Gen Zs are feeling today. But you will get it from a positive and uplifting perspective.

The insights in this book are transformative.

Zachary and Sofia received assistance from the TIEF board, which is made up of fourteen members with diverse backgrounds. The board includes distinguished experts in special education and school psychology, including university professors from several countries. The members come from the United States, Britain, Romania, Poland, and Cameroon.

TIEF believes this book will substantially benefit students, parents, educators, and the general public. I welcome you to embrace and spread the ideas in this book, **Business for a Better World: The Gen Z Guide to Profit and Purpose**.

Sally A. Baas

President of Tapestry Intergenerational Education Foundation

INTRODUCTION

This book offers you a powerful framework shaped by successful business entrepreneurs and written by me, a seventeen-year old, in order to make it accessible for the new set of Gen Z students. I wanted to write the book because I've always been interested in business, but I struggled to understand what exactly it entails. So I did lots of research to better understand it. I interviewed business leaders. And I spent lots of time thinking about concepts to turn these ideas into practically useful, understandable tools for others. Although "business" may seem like a hefty word, I've realized that there are a few essentials.

I hope to offer you fresh ideas so you can understand the keys to business and even make this word a friendly word to use. It is my dream to change this word to one of success, new revelations, technology, and so much more.

For too long, business has been seen as the trade shaped by ambition and rewards. But I believe that business is best done when you serve the interests of the buyer, seller, and society. In other words, business can be good for everyone.

I thought my thinking was unique...but then I discovered a fascinating philosophy of some of the most successful business people in the world. They were from Japan and lived in the sixteenth century. They were called Omi Merchants. You probably have never heard of them. They believed that the most effective approach to business is to keep three stakeholders satisfied at the same time - sellers, buyers, and society. People trusted them because they were not out for greed. They cared as much for society as for the buyer or seller.[1]

That's why I call this book *Business for a Better World*.

WHY READ THIS BOOK?

Everyone needs business skills. Our day to day lives require lots of business skills from budgeting to management, leadership to marketing — some of the most important skills for thriving in our world. Yet they are rarely integrated into the school curriculum. *Very rarely*. Youth need to learn why business is important, how to create a business, and how to love the process. There are plenty of business experts out there who can teach us, some whom I've talked to. This book is about what they have to say as well as what I have learned from them, from my own research, and the jobs I've taken on.

I'm writing this book to address the importance of business to us as Gen Zs. Our generation has some of the most creative thinkers and innovators, and I hope this book can help us reach our individual and collective potential. We can make the world a better place through the power of business.

I will introduce you to what I call The Four Insights, the things that are most important in business and in life. An insight is a behavior that helps you become a better problem-solver, forward-thinker, and Gen Zer who can make informed decisions. Many business books have valuable insights. Mine are unique. Other business books focus on market dynamics, financial analytics, and customer behavior. But

1 For more information on the Omi Shonin Merchants, see the scholarship of Professor Jiro Tamura, Keio University. Here are details: Jiro Tamura, A Comparative Analysis of Harvard and Japanese Style Negotiation: Preparation Using the 5-Step SMATO Approach, 94(6) Journal of Law, Politics, and Sociology 45, 49 (2021; in Japanese).

those ideas are from experts you don't know and most likely not Gen Zs. But through me - though my writing may not be perfect - you'll want to learn business.

My insights will guide you. Whether or not you're interested in business, these can be a positive tool for you, no matter what you end up doing in life. These insights include having a positive mindset, learning financial awareness, decoding your society, and understanding competition. I'm going to show you how to understand all of this to become somewhat of an expert.

No one can live without business. It's part of everything we do. I get upset when others talk about business as though it's a selfish act. It's not. Business is what makes the world go round.

Think about how business affects your own life. By the end of this book, you will see how it influences all aspects of your life. Once you know how business works, it empowers you to become a modern day Omi Shonin merchant. You will be able to utilize business to improve your own circumstances, that of business partners, and that of the world. In short, you will know how to use business to promote a better world.

Ready to start? Let's dive in!

PART I: THE PROBLEM

Business For A Better World

CHAPTER ONE: WHY BUSINESS IS IMPORTANT TO EVERYONE

You may wonder why a seventeen-year-old is writing a book on business. We - as Gen Zs - are the future of a huge world. How we think is important. Someday, we are going to be the adults in the room. Now, that might seem far off, but it's the truth. We are going to be the ones making the big decisions. We are the ones who need to trust others so we must be trustworthy, too. Yes, it's all about you and me.

Why Is Business Important?

First, everything around us is somehow connected to business. We live in a democracy, and business is what is possible to buy and sell. If you drink water, someone in business helped to make the water run into your home. If you go to school, some business person may have contributed money to your school. If you read books at school (and I assume you do), someone got paid to write the books and publishing houses made money selling them. Or if you eat food in the school cafeteria, a business supplied the school with that food. Even the school building itself was built by business people. We call them investors, architects, authors, farmers - but they all are dealing with aspects of business. So it's about all of us. No one is excluded. We all need to understand how business works.

Second, everyone has to make decisions about how to spend money. You might get an allowance, or your parents might hand you a $10 bill and tell you to go buy something. So, you have to think about how you'd spend it. Or you may be the leader in your class and you are going to have a food drive to help the homeless and you have to think about the cost. Even coming up with a family budget requires business understanding.

Third, business teaches you important life skills. Business skills allow you to see the world through a broader lens, so that you are prepared for situations that are hard to deal with. You learn how to solve problems, communicate effectively, manage money, and take on greater responsibilities. It doesn't matter what field you want to pursue; business skills will help.

Those reasons got me thinking. I remember sitting at my computer one day and wondering how my grandfather became a successful businessman. He was once seventeen. Did he know what he wanted to do back then? How did he learn how to manage money?

Another day, a friend headed to college said he was going to major in business. I thought about it and asked myself, "What should I do with my life?" I've always been intrigued by business, but I've not been quite sure what it is all about. Did you ever have that kind of feeling about something?

Most of my friends don't know much about business. We don't take courses at school. People on-line try to get me interested in business, but it often feels dangerous and fake. So I've taken it upon myself to learn more, and to have you learn with me. My goal is to learn alongside you about business. Together as Gen Zs, I am confident we can create a better world.

Time flies, so does business

Let's think about how business has changed. This gives us a historical perspective.

A simple example is to ask your grandparents what shopping was like fifty years ago and how it has changed today. What did they do to get their needs met back then? If your grandparents are like mine, they will say that they went to small stores around the corner. This was before shopping malls. Then the shopping malls appeared, and you probably remember those. My Nana said they would walk the malls, meet friends, and shop in the stores.

Now, looking at today's world, it's all on-line shopping. Businesses do not even need to contact customers face-to-face when selling. This is a major change affecting the quality of products bought by customers. Consider how easy customers can buy items now and how business markets effectively make people buy faster on-line.

Think about running a business today. You need to deal with the complexity of building and running a business when confronted with fake social media, or AI. It's nothing like what our grandparents experienced! There are vastly different norms across generations and cultures.

As a kid, I thought business was so simple! Just come up with an idea and do it. But as I've grown up, I've found out there is so much more to creating a flourishing business. While you read this book, I will show you how to take these steps. It's not that I know it all. I'm just thinking it through like a normal Gen Z'er and offering new ways to think about business for a better world.

CHAPTER TWO: THE FOUR INSIGHTS - YOUR KEYS TO SUCCESS

When I started researching how to achieve business success, I was overwhelmed. Business is complicated. But then I started to see patterns to business success. I realized there are a few essential components to this thing we call business. In fact, I've broken down business success into four components that I call **Insights**.

Each insight is a lens that helps you see different important parts of business success. Once you look through the lens of an Insight, you will be surprised at how much more you will understand the world of business. These Insights focus on the two key sides of business: creating value and dealing with people. Keeping these in mind ensures you act on the Omi Shonin philosophy, doing good for the buyers, sellers, and the world.

The rest of the book explores the Four Insights. I will tell you stories and give you skills to help you think like a business person. You will learn how to see the world –and your life–through the lens of each Insight. These Insights are the foundation of business success. Once you know them, you will understand how to create a budget, how to lead a team, and how to be a good manager. These principles are foundational to personal development and social awareness, and I believe they are key to the lens of your own imagination.

My approach is to give you not only the tools you need to understand business, but the underlying principles that can help you live the philosophy of effective business people. So, for example, you will learn not just how to put together a budget but also how to stay disciplined; and you'll do so through the eyes of a kid who thinks like you do.

Through these Insights, I'm giving you what I believe are **practical skills** to create value and helping you to build your **emotional intelligence** through my experiences. By applying these Insights, you will vastly improve your ability to be effective in business. It's all through the eyes of a real Gen Z.

PART II: THE STRATEGY
- THE FOUR INSIGHTS -

CHAPTER THREE: INSIGHT #1 - ELEVATE YOUR MINDSET

Elevate Your Mindset

Insight One:
Elevate Your Mindset

In between school, scrolling, and zoning out, have you ever paused to ask yourself, *"How do I actually think?"* Probably not. Most of us don't. But if you're not careful, your thoughts can make you unproductive. And that is a really big problem in business.

If your thoughts feel cloudy or you get consumed in negativity, don't just bear it. Elevate your mindset. Recognize how powerful your mind really is and learn how to use that power to your advantage. Yes, in business you need to manage people, build products, provide services, and cultivate clients. But before you try to change anything out there, start in here, in yourself. With our mindset.

You can't create a good business if your mindset is too narrow. **A well-rounded mindset** helps you stay focused, think creatively, bounce back from failure, and keep going when things get tough. Makes sense, right?

Your mindset is the lens through which you see the world. So before anything else, let's start here - *with you*. Because how can you even begin to think about influencing others if you barely know yourself? In this chapter, I'm going to help you see just how important a well-rounded mindset is in business, and I'm going to share with you a few powerful techniques to elevate your mindset for business success.

MINDSET IS IMPORTANT IN BUSINESS

Your mindset frames how you think, feel, and respond to challenges. A positive mindset sets you on the path to get through tough moments and learn from them. You look at obstacles in business as challenges, not problems. And you approach them with determination, not fear.

Here's the thing: your mindset is a choice. You can choose imagination, creativity, and opportunity - or not. It's up to you. You can elevate your mindset. Take a moment now and ask yourself:

- When something doesn't go as planned, do I shut down...or ask, *"What can I learn from this?"*
- When a new idea feels risky, do I focus on what might go wrong...or what *could* go right?
- Do I look at competitors with envy...or ask, *"What can I learn from them?"*
- When I hear "no," do I stop trying...or think, *"What's my next move?"*
- Do I avoid feedback...*or welcome it to grow?*

If you're saying "yes" to most of these, then it's time to build a stronger mindset. And even if you said no, you can always strengthen your mindset. The best business leaders recognize this and are learning all the time. A **well-rounded mindset** is what will help you become more resilient and guide you to long-term success. So where to begin?

First, recognize the key characteristics of a well-rounded mindset. I've pinpointed a few, but you'll discover others through your own journey. This mindset is open to learning, feedback, and determination. It helps you stay humble enough to improve and confident enough to keep going. These qualities don't just make you better in business. They make you better in life.

Second, pay attention to the thoughts in your head. Mindset starts with self-awareness. What do you tell yourself when things don't go your way? What patterns do you notice in your thinking when you're stressed out? My Dad always says, "Go to the balcony and look

11

down." I used to roll my eyes when he'd tell me that, but honestly? It works. From that balcony, you get some distance. It's not always easy to become aware of your current mindset, but it's totally possible. I know, because I did it. And you can, too.

Third, re-frame how you see business. It's not just about making money. It's about making smart, intentional choices. It's about being honest, understanding people, and offering real value. Even something as simple as babysitting the neighbor's kids teaches you how to earn, spend, and save. It teaches you to value your time, your skills, and your effort. And those lessons compound. They'll help you avoid stress and debt—and build confidence down the road.

Last, business doesn't have to be selfish. In fact, it shouldn't be. It's about creating something that can provide for others, support your community, and stay grounded in honesty. That all begins with mindset. A strong, positive mindset helps you make better decisions, become a better leader, and stick with things when they get hard.

Tools for a Well-Rounded Mindset

So now you're probably asking: How do I actually do this?

Here are the five most important mindset tools I've come up with. I've discovered these through my own experiences at work and in my home life. These aren't just tips from me to you—they're *for you*, and about you.

- **Think strategically**. Consider life as a puzzle, and every piece is shaped differently. You have to consider all other options before you make a move. Same goes in life, you must think big picture with your goal at the top of your priorities.

- **Be flexible on the "how"**. Think about the puzzle again, you are able to put different pieces in a different order even if you did the puzzle 100 times, however you still will get the end result. Use this as a reminder that you can get from point A to point B in many different ways.

- **Lead by example**. Nobody is perfect. Not even close. However everybody has a role model they look up to. Your job is to become someone else's role model, and guide by setting an example for others to follow.

- **Build a collaborative culture**. Being included and valued in any setting promotes collaboration. When you build an environment that promotes people working together, everyone is more likely to be engaged and participate, no matter the scale. This also means making sure people are motivated to work hard, but don't feel so stressed that they suffer mental or physical health issues.

- **Seek feedback**, and use it. Understanding what people want is crucial to innovation and creativity. Remember that new ideas promote change and growth, however it all begins with understanding customer input.

An Example: Google

Let's take a look at how Google seeks to promote each of these five tools for a well-rounded mindset.

You know Google. It's a tech giant. I recognize most of us aren't running billion-dollar companies, but what stands out to me about Google isn't just its products. It's the well-rounded mindset they seek to build at the company. They're not perfect, and I know they've received criticism about some of their practices. But there's still a lot we can learn from the way they operate.

First, think strategically. Google sees the big picture. Their strategic success isn't only based on new tools or tech. They work to make every part of the company fit together to support long-term innovation. They invest in their people, their culture, and their systems with a long game in mind.

Second, be flexible on the "how." Google is known for setting big goals, but they don't always stick to one path to get there. A great example is how they approached communication tools. They aimed to create a product that helped people connect and collaborate, but their first attempt, Google Wave, didn't take off. Instead of giving up, they tried again with Google Hangouts. Then, as needs changed, they tried again, developing Google Meet and Chat as part of their workspace suite. The strategic goal stayed the same—a communication tool—but the "how" kept evolving. That showed me that it's okay if my first idea doesn't work. What matters is staying committed to the purpose while being open to new ways of getting there.

Third, lead by example. Google tries to build a culture in which leaders set the tone through action. Their leaders don't just talk about values like openness, curiosity, and respect. They seek to model them every day. Whether it's a manager seeking input from junior team members or an executive admitting they don't have all the answers, collaboration and innovation start with humility. That showed me that leadership isn't only about power—it's about role modeling how to work together and keep growing.

Fourth, build a collaborative culture. One of the things I respect most about Google is how much they value collaboration. Mentorships, cross-team projects, retreats, and open communication all help them build a sense of community. That made me think differently about the people I surround myself with. Whether I'm working on a group project or just going through life, having a collaborative environment can completely change my motivation to work hard on a project.

Fifth, seek feedback, and use it. Google is known for its feedback culture. Employees are encouraged to give and receive input regularly, and they're expected to act on it. I used to get nervous hearing feedback, like it was a sign I failed. But seeing how Google builds it into their growth process made me realize feedback is a tool for personal and company growth. Whether I get feedback from teachers, friends, or teammates, I try to listen to it and take it into consideration. It's not always easy, but it's made me a better person.

IN SUM: ELEVATE YOUR MINDSET

Congratulations! You've just learned how to create a thriving mindset! Your state of mind determines how you make sense of events that happen day to day—and how you lead. Taking control of your mindset allows you to roll with setbacks rather than dreading them, and it empowers you to build your business with greater energy and focus.

The big idea: A good mindset prioritizes business success by encouraging you to:

1. Think strategically.
2. Be flexible on the "how."
3. Lead by example.
4. Build a collaborative culture.
5. Seek feedback, and use it.

With all of this in mind, **let's explore Insight #2**.

15

WORKSHEET #1: TRY IT OUT

Practicing the 5 Tools for a Well-Rounded Mindset

Now that you understand how these five tools of a well-rounded mindset work at Google, I want you to practice applying them to sharpen your understanding of them and to get better at using them.

Here's the situation: Imagine you're the CEO of a small business called **Fresh Smoothie Gen Z** - known in short as **Fresh Smoothie** - a smoothie and juice cart that sets up near schools and parks. You want to serve healthy, affordable drinks and snacks to students and families. Let's see how you'd build and lead this business using the 5 mindset tools.

1. Think Strategically.

Sales at Fresh Smoothie are slow on rainy days. What are 3 possible ways to handle this?

1.

2.

3.

Which idea would you choose - and why?

2. Be Flexible on the "How"

Your goal is to attract more customers after school. What are 2 creative options to help Fresh Smoothie stay open on rainy days? (Examples: You could locate near stores where people are inside. You could sell umbrellas. Etc.)

Idea A:

Idea B:

3. Lead Like They're Watching

Choose 3 leadership qualities you want to model as the boss of Fresh Smoothie:

1.

2.

3.

Pick one and explain how you'll show it in action: I will show _____ by _____

_____

4. Build a Collaborative Culture

• What is one possible strategy to build collaboration?

5. Seek Feedback—and Use It

• What's one question you'd ask customers about Fresh Smoothie? How will you use that information?

•

• What's one question you'd ask employees about Fresh Smoothie? How will you use that information?

CHAPTER FOUR: INSIGHT #2 - MASTER THE MECHANICS

Insight Two:
Master the Mechanics

Master the Mechanics

Now that we have a strong mindset, we can begin to look closer at *actual business itself.* What is a business?

Business is the exchange of one kind of value for another. If I'm going to buy your bike, I give you money and you give me the bike. We have exchanged one type of value for another: I get the bike, and you get equal value through the money I give you to purchase it. Easy, right?

Not at all. Business is complicated, especially if you create a company. Business owners need to know so much stuff, but it's so hard to know what to specifically focus on. Every business has money moving in and out. Customers are lost and customers are gained. You have spreadsheets, accounting, marketing, and trying to manage the people in your company while catering to the customers and on and on. It's overwhelming! But if you don't master the mechanics things can go wrong, FAST. I know a company in my hometown that busted a worker for stealing some of its products. They never would have known if the owner hadn't studied the spreadsheets. You have to master the mechanics!!!

But what are the most important factors to master the mechanics? My answer: RC^2. Before I tell you what the RC^2 is, I want you to take a guess. Don't worry if you are wrong. My hint: it represents four words that are essential for knowing the mechanics..

Give it a try now. What are two words that start with "R" and are the most important in business? I'll give you ten, and you choose the two that you think I chose.

Return

Resilience

19

Resources

Risk

Reputation

Retention

Revenue

Responsibility

Regulation

Research

Now try the same with the two "C" words.

Creativity

Communication

Collaboration

Commitment

Consistency

Customers

Competence

Capital

Change

Cost

Here are my answers. RC² stands for **Risk, Revenue, Customers, and Collaboration**. These are basic mechanics you need to make money (revenue), serve the right people (customers), navigate uncertainty, (risk) and work with others to make it all happen (collaboration). If you know these, you will be in a good place for business success.

THE MECHANICS OF BUSINESS

Remember these four mechanics and get ready to try them out later in the chapter.

Let's start with **Revenue**. This is the money your business earns from selling its product or service. In simple terms: No revenue, no business. What are you selling, how much does it cost to make, who do you have to pay for help, and how can you make a profit? Remember profit is different from revenue: Revenue is all the money you earn. Profit is what's left after you pay your costs to employees, to pay for products, and so on..

Next is **Risk**. You can't grow a business without taking chances, but you have to understand the stakes. Some people take great risks in business and it pays off; others fail and learn from it. There are many types of risk: financial, reputation, and the time and energy you invest that could have gone elsewhere.

The third mechanic is **Customers.** Your customers are the lifeline of your company. Without customers, what's the point? You will make no profit, no revenue, no company. You need to understand, attract, and keep customers. So you really need to know who your product is for, and what needs of theirs this will fulfill.

The fourth is **Collaboration**. You need everyone *inside the company* to work well together. Otherwise, you don't work as efficiently, and as a result, customers notice and move elsewhere to get their needs met. Think about all moving parts inside a business, such as coordinating roles, schedules, strengths, and communication. Everyone has to be in sync to make sure everything works in sync.

YOUR TURN: THINKING ABOUT RC2

Thinking of RC^2 in relation to a lemonade stand is fairly simple. But you can use it in more complicated business contexts, too. Pretty much any business can be broken down using the RC2. Let's give it a try. I want you to create your own business. Answer the questions on the **"Business Plan Worksheet"** to help you build it.

YOUR TURN: THE LEMONADE STAND

Let's go through it with the RC^2 concept.

Name your Lemonade Stand: _____

The Four Mechanics	Question	Your Answer
R – REVENUE	Imagine each cup of lemonade is *$3*. You sell 100 cups of lemonade each day. It costs *$0.50* to buy the cups and lemonade powder. What is your profit per day? This is revenue minus costs.	
R – RISK	What could go wrong with your lemonade stand?	

The Four Mechanics	Question	Your Answer
C – CUSTOMERS	Who are your customers? (Kids? Adults? Neighbors? Walkers?)	
	How will you attract them? (Signs? Smiles? Social media? Word of mouth?)	
	Do you offer anything special? (Flavors, ice-cold drinks on a hot day, extra-friendly service?)	
	How will you keep them coming back?	
C-COLLABORATION	Who could help you run your stand? (Siblings, friends, parents?	
	How can you all work together better? (Schedules, clear communication, sharing profits?)	

Reflection Questions

• What did this activity teach you about running a business?

• How could you use RC2 to support a different business idea? Describe it below.

BUSINESS PLAN WORKSHEET

A. Business Basic

1. What's the name of your business

2. What is your business's key service or product:

B. Revenue

3. How much will you charge for one item or service:

4. How many items or services do you think you can sell per day (on average):

5. How much money will you make in a week? (*Tip*: Multiply the price of one item by how many you think you'll sell in a week.)

C. Risk

6. What are two things that could go wrong or challenge your business:

7. What can you do to prevent these problems:

D. Customers

8. Who do you want to buy your product or service:

9. Describe characteristics of your customers, such as age, hobbies, where they live, etc.

10. How will you let them know about your business and get them to buy from you?

E. Collaboration

11. Who can help you build your business?

12. How will each person help you? What will they do?

13. How will you locate employees to help you run your business

CHAPTER FIVE: INSIGHT #3 - CONNECT TO CONSUMERS

Connect to Consumers

Insight Three:
Connect to Consumers

Businesses want to serve customers faster and better, but they often don't do that very well. They become disconnected from the customer's reality, building products based on poor assumptions about the customers. Business executives work out of offices that are separate from the customer's world. And they lose sight of what the customers really care about. In this chapter, we'll look at how you can close this gap.

My strategy is simple: Connect to consumers. There are two main ways to go about this. One is to get your business's message out. The other is to bring in the voices of consumers to help you tailor your product to their needs. In this chapter, I'll share practical ways to put into practice each of these approaches for connecting to consumers. Let's look at both of these strategies in detail.

GETTING YOUR MESSAGE OUT

The first strategy is to get your message out. You need consumers to know your product exists, what it is all about, and how it will help them. Why should they want to buy your product? Have you ever watched an advertisement and thought it was so entertaining but forgot what they sold? Well, I have. And I don't want you to make that mistake.

This leads us into our first way to connect to consumers: Create a clear brand that reflects what consumers want, not just what you want. A brand is the unique identity of your product or service. Imagine you are selling a plain t-shirt; it might not go for much. But if you throw a Nike logo on the shirt, the price suddenly shoots upward of $40. This is the power of a strong brand. In short, remember to spend the time building a solid brand that fosters trust, style, and status.

A second way to get your service into the consumers' hands is word of mouth. You want to create events that get people talking about your product. It doesn't matter if you are a small shop in a small town or a franchise that retails all over the world, what matters is how you promote yourself and engage in your community. Now, depending on what type of business you are in, you can host events with partner organizations or even bring in celebrities to help build excitement and gain attention. All of this makes customers perceive your company as useful or trendy. The goal is to spark community engagement and get people talking about your ideas.

A third method I want to mention is charity work and giveaways. Both of these methods help consumers build a positive image of your company and, as a result, more people trust your business. Charity work allows consumers to see that you aren't a greedy organization but rather an active and helpful part of your community. Giveaways help promote your name and allow you to show up at places customers care about without the customers needing to spend money.

There is a recurring theme I want you to notice. Any marketing action you take can either positively or negatively affect your brand. Think about Apple. They have built a powerful brand. When the majority of people think about the company, a positive image comes to mind. The lesson: Your brand is the core of what you do and how people perceive your entire company. So give a lot of thought to marketing your product or service. And keep the Omi Shonin philosophy in mind. Remember these merchants? They only traded when it was good for self, others, and society. And they were the most trusted merchants of their time.

On this note, let's begin to look at ways to use the consumer's voice to better a business.

28

GETTING THE CONSUMER'S MESSAGE IN

Companies often overlook the importance of getting consumer feedback. But ignoring the customer's interests can be fatal, putting the business out of business. A great example of a company not responding to the customers' urge for innovation was Blockbuster. Whether you know the company or not, it is useful to learn from. Blockbuster was a store where you could go in and rent DVDs. They took over the movie rental industry and boomed. However, they went bankrupt in 2010. What went wrong? Blockbuster executives failed to adapt to the trending digital streaming industry, which millions of customers indicated was more convenient and appealing. This led average consumers to stop renting Blockbuster's products. Blockbuster learned the hard way that if you don't listen to customer feedback - and then innovate—your company is at risk. Big risk.

The following are three methods to learn from your consumers.

The first method revolves around an idea so simple, it might sound silly, but trust me, it works. Talk to everyday customers and ask for their recommendations on how to improve the product or service. Organize "focus groups" and ask them about the product's strengths and weaknesses. What advice do they have? Although simple, remember to do this. You need to get customer input to make smart changes to your marketing strategy and to make innovative changes to your product.

The second method is something most companies do. Have you ever purchased something and received an email to fill out a survey? The company is trying to amass as much data as possible to help them decide how to improve their product and better the customer experience. Surveys are an amazing way to gather data because they are quick, requiring little effort to do and resulting in lots of useful information.

29

The last method is to take the feedback and tweak your product or service in response to the consumer's interests. This takes an open mind. Too many companies spend lots of time developing their product, so they are not too open to feedback. But that's a mistake. Successful companies excel at maintaining a product's strengths while carefully modifying it to the consumer's desires.

These three ways, if applied correctly, allow you to take in feedback and change your products based on it. Remember: listening to your consumers is just as important as finding new ones. Customers are more likely to come back when they see innovation based on their changing needs. Taking in information and sending your message out are equally important, and a well-structured business will utilize both approaches.

Now let's look at a great example of a company that knows how to market: Nike.

NIKE: Masters of Connecting to Consumers

Nike is one of the greatest comeback stories of all time. Years back, they were on the edge of collapse, but they turned their company around by connecting really effectively to consumers. Let's look at how the company used both sides of my strategy: getting the message out and bringing the consumer's voice in.

Nike created a powerful brand that spoke to motivation and individuality, as represented in their slogan "Just Do It." They created a new trend and designed stylish athletic wear that fit into the growing health lifestyle. Nike also utilized word-of-mouth marketing and community engagement by sponsoring local sports programs and promoting diversity and inclusion in athletics. This built trust around their brand. And Nike strengthened its public image through charity work, from promoting sustainability with recycled materials to encouraging physical activity in under-served communities. This made Nike a brand that people saw as caring about society.

At the same time, Nike excelled at getting the consumer's message in. First, they listened to customers and encouraged them to share their experiences and stories. This informed the further development and marketing of their products. They also gathered feedback and tracked buying habits. Customers could even design their own sneakers, giving them a sense of ownership. Finally, Nike recognized that its consumers cared about the environment and were worried about climate change. So they offered sustainable product lines. By letting customer values shape their innovations, Nike kept their products relevant and kept their consumers loyal.

So, you can see that Nike is a good example of a brand that thrives by sending a clear, powerful message out AND actively pulling the consumer's voice in to shape future products.

Practice helps. On the next page is a worksheet to complete to learn how to connect with consumers.

SUMMARY

This chapter focused on two main ideas. Getting your message out and taking consumers' messages in. The three strategies to get your message out are: (1) create a clear brand identity, (2) utilize word of mouth marketing, and (3) engage in charity work and giveaways. Also remember the three strategies to take in the consumer's perspective: (1) conduct focus groups for feedback, (2) implement surveys to gather customer insights, and (3) adapt products based on consumer interests.

Using these six strategies will promote entrepreneurial growth and will allow your product to adapt to the world's never-ending desires.

WORKSHEET #3 YOUR TURN: CONSUMER CONNECTION WORKSHEET

Instructions: You are going to create a new company and develop ways to connect your product to consumers.

Your company sells what? _____

Now use the 6 strategies below to plan how to connect to consumers.

Getting Your Message Out

1. Clear brand

   a. Who are your target consumers?

   b. What is your brand?

   c. How does your brand connect to the consumers?

2. Word of mouth strategy:

   a. How will you get people talking about your product or service?

   b. What events or partnerships will you plan?

3. Charity work and community engagement

a. How will you show you care about more than just profits?

b. What cause could you support that fits your brand?

Bringing the Customer's Voice In

4. Customer Feedback

a. How will you get customers to share their thoughts, stories, and reviews?

5. Behavioral Feedback

a. How will you observe what customers actually buy?

b. How will you use this information?

6. Adapting to Trends

a. What big trends will you watch for—such as sustainability, diversity, or technology trends?

b. How might you adjust your product based on these trends

CHAPTER SIX: INSIGHT #4 - EXCEL THROUGH COMPETITION

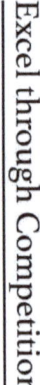
Excel through Competition

Insight Four:
Excel through
Competition

Believe it or not, I learned a key business concept through a playful game of ping pong with my older brother, Noah. We were in the basement hitting the ball back and forth, all while talking to each other and having a nice conversation. At first, it was lots of fun and stress-free. But once we started to keep score and play games to eleven, it got tense. The score was 9 to 9, and it felt like we were in the Olympics. I had the serve and threw it up—and missed the table. I clenched my paddle and hit the table in frustration. Noah looked on and said, "Nice try, buddy!"

Now I was *determined* to win. With the game on the line, he served and it barely scratched the table. And just like that, I lost. It stung like a bee bite, and I was tempted to throw my paddle at the floor. Now I was determined to get better so I could rematch him and WIN.

Over many months, I practiced—and started to win. Not all the time, but more often. Unfortunately, this also pushed Noah to practice more and get better. But the big takeaway is clear: competition pushed both of us to get better.

The purpose of this chapter is to help you understand the benefits of competition in business. I'll also show you how to excel through competition by building a powerful value proposition.

COMPETITION MATTERS

The fourth insight is to **excel through competition**. What is competition? It is when you and another business try to achieve the same goal, but only one can win. Think about Noah and me in ping pong; only one of us could win the game. In business, we compete over everything from getting more customers to making better products and gaining attention on social media.

Competition can make or break your company. It keeps companies on their toes and forces them to innovate to maintain their business and gain more consumers. Remember, competition never goes away unless your business fails. So you might as well learn how to use it well.

I want to look closer at two companies that compete with each other, *Apple* and *Samsung*. My dad has stuck with the *Samsung* phone and I have stuck with the newest *Apple* device. I always ask him why he can't just be *normal* and buy an *iPhone*. I'm sure my dad and I will never come to full agreement on which is better, even though I know it's the *iPhone*! But in reality, the answer is more complicated. And I have to admit: it takes lots of guts to not stand with *Apple*. But that's besides the point.

Apple has a few qualities that differentiate it from *Samsung*: It has an integrated ecosystem with the *iPhone*, *iPad*, and *Apple Watch*, creating a family of products that seem easy to buy and understand how to use. *Apple* uses media coverage that focuses on their products and holds launch events that get people excited for a product release. These ideas together are just a glimpse at what *Apple* does to distinguish itself from the competition.

But *Samsung* also has some unique qualities that make it competitive in the market. It prioritizes a broad range of devices at various price points, catering to various consumer interests. In their marketing, they bring in top celebrities like soccer star Lionel Messi and sponsor major events that generate views.

Apple and *Samsung* use different marketing strategies to gain an edge over each other. They each take a unique focus on innovation, marketing, and the customer experience. Their deep investment in research drives continuous improvement, helping them stay at the top of the technology sector – and ultimately getting more business for their company. **That's competition at work.**

THE POWER OF HEALTHY COMPETITION

You might think competition in business is just about getting ahead of others, but it's so much deeper than that. When you're in business, you're not just selling a product or service. You're challenging yourself to do better every single day. Without competition, where's the drive to improve? Where's the push to evolve and innovate? When I teach basketball lessons to kids and tell them to just "go clean the gym," they slack off and take their sweet time. But the moment I say, "First one to pick up the cones wins," suddenly everyone's hustling. Why? Because competition *motivates*. It forces us to show up, think bigger, and do better. It's the same in business.

Without competition, businesses would stay stagnant: no new ideas would surface, no fresh strategies would emerge, and customers would get bored. Competition is what forces businesses to compete for attention, market share, and talent. Think of it this way: competition is the driving force that makes you stronger.

But not all parts of the competition are bright. Unchecked competition can quickly become harmful. If businesses are too focused on beating others at all costs, they might sacrifice quality, customer satisfaction, or even ethical practices. The pressure to outdo competitors can lead to dangerous decisions like cutting corners to save costs, which ultimately can hurt the brand. When businesses start to focus more on beating the competition than creating value, the entire market can suffer. Competition should be a force that drives growth, not one that leads to reckless decisions or unsustainable practices.

The best example I know of how competition helps companies grow is the rivalry between *Coke* and *Pepsi*. They have an iconic rivalry dating back to the late nineteenth century. It reminds me of my own epic rivalry with my brother Noah. *Coke* was created in 1886, with *Pepsi* following in 1893. As they grew independent, they competed fiercely for market share.

In the mid-20th century, both companies used aggressive advertising and marketing strategies. *Coke* focused on classic branding around themes of happiness. In fact, my great-uncle Peter Sealey was the marketing head at Coca Cola years ago and thought up the famous polar bear concept that rocketed *Coke* to new heights of appeal. *Pepsi*, on the other hand, focused on targeting younger customers with celebrity endorsements to gain legitimacy and traction. Both companies innovated products and campaigns to attract customers.

THE BILLION-DOLLAR VALUE PROPOSITION

I want you to think about any item you have purchased—maybe a computer, poster, or candy bar. Now, determine what edged you toward buying that product rather than others? Was it the simple design, more intriguing packaging, cheaper cost, or better social media ad? Whatever the reason, that is **your value proposition**. That right there single-handedly is the company's weapon to outdo competition.

What's a value proposition?

A value proposition is a clear statement that explains why a customer should choose your product or service over others. It highlights the unique benefits you offer. The stronger your value proposition, the more likely customers will use your business. Still, it's also important to understand your competitors' value proposition because it helps you shape your market strategy and stand out in the market.

Imagine you are CEO of a tech company and your biggest competition begins to surpass your business in sales. The problem seems large at first, but upon researching, you see they have begun to change their target market toward younger people, knowing they are more likely to purchase technology products. They changed their packaging. On the outside, it features a more modern, slick design. Their stores changed product placement to put more emphasis on easier-to-buy stuff. And they upgraded the lights and music systems to market toward younger buyers. And they also improved the *customer experience* by putting their technologies on the shelves and allowing customers to test them.

All of these changes boosted the rival company's value proposition. And all of this is important for you and your company to know as you try to figure out how to recapture more of the market for your company.

Building a Value Proposition: The 5 Steps

Now, let's learn the five steps to build a value proposition. We're answering the question of what will make customers gravitate toward your product or service.

1. **What need is your product addressing?** Identify the specific problem or unmet desire your product or service solves. You can use surveys, interviews, or focus groups to gather insights from your intended customers. Analyze competitors to find gaps in their offerings. Where can you stand out and deliver more value?

2. **What makes it unique?** Ask yourself what features or benefits set your product apart from competitors. Do you have a unique selling proposition that speaks to a customer's specific need? Compare your product to similar options in the market and highlight what makes your product distinctive, such as superior service, innovation, or convenience.

3. **How does the customer benefit?** Focus on the improvements your product brings to the customer's life. What concrete outcomes do they gain by choosing you over a competitor? Use clear and concise language to communicate the benefits.

4. **How can you prove your product works**? Establish credibility by showing evidence that your product delivers results. Use things like testimonials, success stories, and credentials to back up your claim. Share real experiences and use the recognition of your brand to build trust and remind the customer of the value of your product.

5. **Is your product priced appropriately**? Evaluate the pricing strategy in relation to the value you provide. How does it compare to competitors? Can you clearly communicate the return on investment or the quality in relation to the cost? Aligning your price with its benefits justifies the cost and makes the price tag clear and understandable to potential customers.

Let's say you're thinking about how best to sell a new meal delivery service that focuses on organic ingredients and sustainability. Using the Five Steps, you define your service's value proposition:

First, you identify your potential **customers' needs**. You realize that busy consumers want healthy, sustainable meals but don't have time to cook or find quality ingredients. After that, you think about your service's **unique offering**. In this case, your company delivers 100% organic, locally sourced meals customizable to individual dietary needs. After some research, you learn that no other company has that exact offering. Next, you consider how your service benefits **customers**. You talk with community members and learn they enjoy convenient, nutritious food that aligns with their health goals and that is environmentally friendly. Then, you work on how to give **social proof** that your service works. You build a website, and the homepage says, "Join our community of over 1,000 satisfied customers who have transformed their eating habits with our service." Lastly, you do lots of research on pricing of similar products and decide on a **fair price** that includes things that make the pricing even better, like free delivery over $50 and no hidden fees.

By going through these Five Steps, you clarify why your product and experience is worth the cost - *from the customer's viewpoint*. Remember, your service must be worth it for the buyer to buy it. You want to create value in their lives. You also want to make sure your product is unique and special in comparison to your competitors.

Revisit your value proposition every month or so. Think about how your company can adapt to the ever-changing needs of customers. We all change our interests over time. Reflect on your own life. Are you as interested in buying the older models of *iPhone's* today as you were when they first came out? In our quickly evolving society, markets and customer needs change. So keep thinking about the value proposition.

Value proposition in Action: Starbucks vs Dunkin'

I want to look at how two powerhouse coffee brands, *Starbucks* and *Dunkin'*, differentiate themselves through unique value propositions that try to win over distinct customer groups.

To begin, think about *Starbucks'* and its simplistic, flashier design. *Dunkin'*, on the other hand, may come off as more rugged-looking with colors that are tackier. *Dunkin'* uses colors like pink and orange to stand out and give it a more eye-catching look. *Starbucks*, on the other hand, comes off as modern and keeps things low profile. Each store appeals to a different type of person. *Dunkin'* attracts lower- to middle- class customers while *Starbucks* attracts middle- to upper-class consumers.

Why is this? Because each company creates a different type of *emotional experience* directed toward the consumers it is hoping to attract.

Both companies are successful, but they offer completely different experiences—and that's the point. *Starbucks* isn't trying to win over *Dunkin's* base, and *Dunkin'* isn't trying to mimic *Starbucks*. They each understand their market, speak its language, and create their value proposition accordingly.

In 2023, **Starbucks generated $35.98 billion in revenue**, while **Dunkin' followed with $11.9 billion** - proving there's room for different value propositions to succeed when well executed.

Business Disruption: The Best Value Proposition

There is a very powerful way to outdo the competition in business: Disruption. It sounds like a big word at first. But the idea is quite simple.

Markets can either stay the same or exponentially change. A disruption is the process of *completely* changing the outlook of a specific product or service. The new product is groundbreaking and tends to leave companies doing things "the old way" in the dust. Disruptors challenge traditional business models and create new ones that offer more efficient or profitable services.

A great example of this is *Airbnb*. When a 10% increase in AirBnb listings in a city occurs, it leads to the hotels losing 2-3% revenue - a *major* hit!

Airbnb's disruption is a real-world example of the benefit of creating a value proposition that disturbs markets and outdoes competitors. Sure, you can create a product that adds slight value to people's lives. But if you have an idea that disrupts a market, you will have an indisputable advantage. In *Airbnb's* case, their disruption led to a company now worth billions of dollars – and providing lots of value to its customers.

I believe you can come up with the idea for the next billion-dollar company that can have a big and positive impact on the world. Imagine if your product or service could disrupt a market, solve a real problem, and make the world a better place? Right after this chapter, I created a worksheet for you to complete so that you can dream up the next high-impact company with an amazing and disruptive value proposition that changes the world for the better.

SUMMARY

Now, you have learned lots of what customers value. Knowing this value, **you can use it to create a thriving business that can help your customers and help the world**. The main point to remember is that competition sparks innovation, motivation, and adaptation. You can outwit competitors and better serve your customers by creating a really strong value proposition. That all boils down to five questions to answer: what's your customer's need, what makes your product unique, how does the customer benefit, how can you prove your product works, and is your pricing reasonable? And lastly, remember to disrupt the market as much as I disrupted my brother Noah.

WORKSHEET #4

Your Turn: Disrupting the Market for a Better World

In this worksheet, you'll invent a business idea and walk through the five essential steps to create a strong value proposition that can convince customers to choose your company over others.

Step 1: What Need Are You Addressing?

- Describe the real-world problem you are trying to solve:

- Who experiences this problem (your target customer)?

- How are people solving this now, and why isn't it good enough?

Step 2: What Makes Your Solution Unique?

- What's your product or service?

- What makes it unique?

Step 3: How Does the Customer Benefit?

- The main benefit to the customer is:

- Here's how their life improves:

Step 4: How Can You Prove It Works?

- Ways I can show my product works (pick at least 2, and describe how you'll do them):
  - ❑ Testimonials
  - ❑ Demos
  - ❑ Case Studies
  - ❑ Endorsements
  - ❑ Certifications
  - ❑ Before & After Results

Step 5: Is the Price Right?

- What's the price of my product, and why that price:
- Compared to competitors, my price is:
  ❑ Higher ❑ Lower ❑ About the same - because:
- Why it's worth the cost:

How Does Your Company Make the World Better?

In one sentence, describe how your company helps people, society, and the planet:

PART III: AN INTERVIEW WITH MY BUSINESS ROLE MODEL

CHAPTER SEVEN: OUR CONVERSATION and REFLECTIONS

LESSONS FROM MY GRANDFATHER

You've made it this far in my book, so you already know the Four Insights: elevate your mindset, master the mechanics, connect to your community, and excel through competition. But these insights aren't just concepts; they are real-life tools. I saw them at work through someone I've admired since I was a kid: my grandfather, or as I call him, PePa.

For many years, he ran a garment manufacturing company Duncannon Dress Factory, which employed 120 people. But before doing that, he was just a kid growing up in a tight-knit working-class neighborhood in Harrisburg, Pennsylvania. Born in 1945, just after World War II, he lived in a row house, in a community with lots of relatives nearby. Life was simple: one TV and two television channels, no air conditioning, and small semi-detached brick homes with connecting front porches. He had a very good life even though he didn't have a lot of material things. And of course, there certainly weren't computers back then. He mowed the grass, rode his bike and played ball with his friends.

I wanted to learn more about my PePa's insights into business. So, I spent many hours interviewing him about his experiences. It turns out he was using the four Insights of my book many years before I came up with these ideas! Here are some of my key takeaways.

Insight #1: Elevate Your Mindset

This insight is about how you think: be strategic, stay flexible, lead by example, work with others, and ask for feedback, and actually use it.

When I asked PePa if he ever thought about doing something *other* than joining the family business, he shook his head. He did go to college and graduate school but then his father wanted him to use his education to expand the family business. "It sounded like a challenge," he told me. "My father wanted me to keep the family business going, and I did it!" That might sound old-school, but what he really meant was to focus, don't overthink everything, and take action when it matters.

He never saw himself as too good for any job. If something needed to be done, he just did it. "I had to be the janitor if he got sick," he said. "I had to pay the bills, take out the garbage, and know where the trucks could park so as not to disturb the neighbors." That's the kind of leadership that inspires people. Running a family business was hard. And he worked hard and did everything that needed to be done.

He also had a great mindset. He didn't panic when things changed. He stayed calm, made adjustments, and helped his employees do the same. He didn't talk about "mindset" or "collaboration." He *lived* it. He modeled care and concern and collaboration with his employees. And because of this, they wanted to work with him, not just for him.

Insight #2: Master the Mechanics (RC²)

This insight focuses on the four business basics: **Risk, Revenue, Customers, and Collaboration**, which I call RC².

PePa didn't run his business from some fancy office. Even though he had many assistants, he liked to keep on top of things. He knew everything about how the place worked…literally. Every step of the production process, from laying out the fabric to sewing, inspecting, packaging and shipping the garments. He explained in detail. "Once the preparatory work was done," he said, "the garments would work their way through an assembly line… Then someone would pack the garments by size and color according to the order." You could tell he respected the process and the people involved in every stage.

And he kept track of the finances with the help of his financial advisor, because as he said, "I had to have a good idea of our cash flow because we had a sizable payroll to meet each week," he said. "Sometimes I would even jot thoughts down on a piece of scrap paper." No spreadsheets. Just sharp instincts and constant awareness.

Risk? He lived it daily. A late shipment to Walmart could mean a lost order. He didn't freak out. He adjusted quickly. He figured out alternatives to meet the deadline.

As for collaboration, he had a system called "piecework - rates." Simply put, you got paid based on how quickly and accurately you worked. "There was a base rate," he explained, "and you could exceed it, but not go lower. That was considered fair at the time." It motivated people without burning them out. That's how you build a system that respects the work and the workers.

Insight #3: Connect to Consumers and Your Community

This one's BIG! Business isn't just about selling something. It's about the people. PePa deeply understood this. You have to know how to share your message and how to actually listen to what your customers and employees are saying, and you need to respond to their needs.

PePa made this look easy. "I treated the employees more like family," he said. "If they were sick or had family issues, and they missed work, we understood. And, we had office parties to get to know each other better." He wasn't just running a company. He was supporting a small town. "The money our employees earned got spent locally. Our business helped support other local businesses, and in reality, it helped the whole community."

He treated customers with the same respect. When I asked if he used contracts, he laughed. "No contracts," he said. "Just a handshake." That one line hit me. His word *was* his contract. His reputation and character were strong enough to keep these customers coming back.

Insight #4: Excel Through Competition

This final insight focuses on your **value proposition**: what makes you different and why should someone choose you over the competition.

PePa wasn't trying to be the biggest company in the country. He focused on being *the best* at what his company did: reliable quality, strong relationships, fair prices, and community impact. That's a clear and compelling value proposition!

He told me what it was like working with big clients. "Sometimes we had to make huge sacrifices to please our top customers," he said. But he never let the company become too dependent on any one customer. "We didn't want to rely on just one client. Having many clients can cause scheduling problems, but we managed to satisfy them all. This is where good communication skills become very important."

He opened a second plant about fifteen miles away. "Eventually, we sold it and returned to focus on expanding the original plant," he said. "Being directly involved allowed me to see things firsthand and to do better financially." That's knowing your limits. That's smart growth.

I asked him what advice he'd give someone my age who wanted to start a business. He said, "If you want to start a business, you need a business plan. You will most likely have to borrow money to start a business, just like a car loan or a mortgage, the bank wants to know how you'll pay it back. Even if you borrow from friends, you need to know how you're going to pay them back and have a profitable business." And then he said a point I find very valuable: "Everything has a price, and if you charge more than your competitors, you better have lower expenses or a 'good name' and branding in your commercial, industrial endeavor."

That's it. That's a value proposition in one sentence: Know what makes your product better than your competition, and then prove it every single day.

What My PePa Taught Me

PePa didn't use buzzwords or business jargon. He just did the work. He showed up early, paid attention to people, treated others fairly, and made smart decisions. And in doing all of that, he lived the Four Insights: he elevated his mindset, mastered the mechanics, connected to the people around him, and competed with integrity.

His final words to me weren't flashy, but they meant everything: "It's important to stay humble and be willing to do whatever it takes to make the business thrive." That's the kind of leader I want to be. And maybe, after reading this, you will too.

PART IV: CONCLUSIONS

CHAPTER EIGHT: CONCLUSION - IT'S YOUR TURN

I want to congratulate you for making it through my Four Insights! But your journey isn't over yet. Now that you understand the big ideas, business will still be no easy feat. It will require hours and hours of daunting and strenuous days for your entrepreneurial dreams to come true. But it can happen!

Whatever path you take in your business adventures, remember the **Four Key Insights**. Let's go over them one last time just the key points.

- **Insight One** challenged us to **elevate our mindset**, reminding us that everything begins with how we think. A growth mindset influences the way we solve problems, lead others, and respond to the inevitable ups and downs. A strong mindset is the foundation not just for business success, but for life.

- **Insight Two** asked us to **master the mechanics** by understanding the core building blocks: Revenue, Risk, Customers, and Collaboration. These are tangible tools that every business, from a lemonade stand to a global brand, must understand to thrive. When you respect the process and stay financially aware, you position yourself to build a long lasting business.

- **Insight Three** taught us to **connect to consumers**. Find ways to incorporate their values, needs, and stories into what you build. We learned that effective business communication goes both ways: sending a message that reflects your brand clearly while staying open to feedback and trends that drive innovation. The best businesses listen more than they speak.

- **Insight Four** urged us to **excel through competition** by refining our value proposition, that unique offering that makes us stand out in a crowded world. Competition allows us to grow, improve, and stay grounded in what sets us apart. We also explored how disruptive ideas can shift entire industries when built with purpose and precision.

Your Turn!

Business is everywhere. It touches every part of our lives. And I've realized that when we're thoughtful, intentional, and bold, business can become one of the greatest tools we have to create a better, more inclusive, and more inspired world.

Here's the thing: I don't want you to simply follow my ideas exactly as they are written. Rather, take them and change them to make them work for you. **Make them better**! This way, they will be more suited to your context and lifestyle.

Finally, don't forget the *philosophy* of my book. As you apply my Four Insights, follow the principles of the Omi Shonin Merchants, who taught us that true business success comes from benefiting the seller, buyer, and society as a whole—all at the same time. By embracing this approach, we can redefine business as a force for good, not greed, and truly create **Business for a Better World**.

Thanks so much for reading my book.

I truly hope it is helpful for you.

No matter where your journey takes you, I want to hear your stories and what entrepreneurial success you find.

Please reach out to me at ZachShapiro4Insights@gmail.com.

ABOUT THE AUTHOR

My name is Zachary Shapiro, but you can call me Zach. I am 17 years old and live in Lexington, Massachusetts, attending Lexington High. I am a rising senior this upcoming year, and like most high school students, I am stressed about my future steps. Over the course of my high school years, I have always loved playing and competing in basketball, one of my true joys in life. In addition, I have spent the past two years researching, writing, and editing this book to help Gen Z better understand the power of business for a better world. If you get to know me, you understand my favorite thing to do when around others is to make people laugh. I hope throughout my career I am able to inspire others, while making a significantly positive impact on our rapidly growing society.